# HOW
# GOD
# WORKS

# HOW GOD WORKS

## HOW IT ALL STARTED AND WHAT TO DO ABOUT IT

### RICHARD SCHINKE

CITI OF
BOOKS

**CITIOFBOOKS, INC.**
3736 Eubank NE Suite A1
Albuquerque, NM 871113579
*www.citiofbooks.com*
Hotline:  1 (877) 3892759
Fax:       1 (505) 9307244

Ordering Information:
Quantity sales. Special discounts are available on quantity purchases by corporations, associations, and others. For details, contact the publisher at the address above.

Printed in the United States of America.

| ISBN13: | Softcover | 979-8-89391-370-5 |
| --- | --- | --- |
| | eBook | 979-8-89391-372-9 |
| | Hardback | 979-8-89391-371-2 |

Library of Congress Control Number: 2024920672

# TABLE OF CONTENTS

# A Foundation

Anyone who has a belief in something must have a basis for that belief, some type of foundation upon which everything else is built. For instance, I belief that the tendency of all physical things is to be drawn to the earth. The word we have for that force is gravity, and I believe in gravity. I believe because I have seen it work 100 percent of the time. As a result, I am careful when I am in high places because I believe that, if I fall from a high place, I will not stop until I reach the bottom, and I will probably die. I also believe that what goes around comes around. The Bible calls it sowing and reaping. Whatever you call it, I believe it to be a true force. That force is the foundation on which I grow my character, and because of that belief, I will tend to help people and not harm them. I know that, if I continually hurt people, people will hurt me.

I have a fundamental belief that the Bible is the Word of God. As a result, my entire spiritual growth is based on the teachings of the Bible. Over the years, I have changed the way I believe about certain spiritual concepts. However, my spiritual foundation, my belief that the Bible is the Word of God, will never change. This belief is just as solid as is my belief in gravity or sowing and reaping. It will never change. Consequently, it is important for me to know the Word of God as well as I can.

Now, although I have this foundational belief— that the Bible is God's Word—I may not always follow its concepts. I may not always do what the Bible instructs me to do. However, I believe I should, and I am not confused about the instructions and principles I find there.

As a result of this foundational belief, I find it logical to believe the principles taught in the Bible. I have read other spiritual books and have found that none can compare to the Bible. As a result, I will not look to other spiritual books to give me true spiritual guidance. Does this sound like I am closed-minded in this area? Absolutely! I have listened to and read enough other possibilities. I have made up my mind and will listen to no more!

So with that as a foundation for this teaching, I will start at the beginning of history, the first book in the Bible, the book of Genesis.

# The Beginning

Adam and Eve were created by God to live and enjoy life on this earth. They weren't born here; they were created. Their story isn't told in a symbolic sort of way so that primitive people could understand that there is a God. Their story is true as written. Adam and Eve were the first people to exist. Think about it; at one point, someone had to be the first people. There had to be a first man and a first woman, and Adam and Eve were those people. They had no human history to learn from because there was no human history. Eve couldn't say "Well, Adam, I cook like this because that is how my mother did it." Eve didn't have a mother! Adam couldn't say "My dad told me to plant the garden in rows and they will grow better." Adam didn't have a dad. They didn't know anything, and they had no past experience to show them how to do things. However, their father, God, was going to teach them all about life and how to do everything.

God gave Adam and Eve a place to live, which was called the Garden of Eden, and told Adam that they could eat anything in the garden except the fruit that grew on the Tree of the Knowledge of Good and Evil. There was another great tree in the garden, and it was called the Tree of Life. God did not tell Adam to not eat from this tree. The implication was that whoever ate from these trees would reap the results of the fruit of the tree. You eat fruit from the Tree of Life, and you have eternal life. You eat fruit from the Tree of the Knowledge of Good and Evil, and you have knowledge of good and evil. I had always found it strange that Adam and Eve didn't eat the fruit from the Tree of Life. They could have eaten all they wanted from that tree, but they didn't. Some have found it strange that God didn't want Adam and Eve to eat the fruit of the Tree of the Knowledge of Good and Evil. Since Satan was on this earth, it would seem like a good idea to know about good and evil. However, Hebrews 5:14 tells us that the knowledge of good and evil is for the mature. Adam and Eve were the very first people on this earth, and they had just been created. They didn't know anything yet. They were adult-looking babies, and they had a lot to learn. God wanted them to get to know him before they went up against Satan. He wanted them to know that he always had their best interest at heart and that his way was always best. They didn't know about Satan, sin, rebellion, or that things could go bad. All they knew was that life was good and that God was always there to help them. They were getting to know him and were gaining a close relationship with him. All they would have had to do was to keep listening to him and to keep following Him. However, they were given free will, and Satan talked them into going against God and eating the fruit from the Tree of the Knowledge of Good and Evil even though God had told them that they would surely die if they did. They didn't even know what death was. They just knew that God had told them to not eat fruit from that tree. They would have done well to just listen to their Father's words. In fact, that is still true today.

# The Entrance of Evil

Evil came into this earth before the creation of man. God had created angels, who were all perfect, followed God, and lived in harmony in the heavens. God wanted the angels to love him, but love can only come if a person or angel has the free will to love or not to love. Love cannot be forced onto anyone. The angel Lucifer was the highest angel in all of creation and led the rest of creation in praise and worship of God. The Bible tells us that Lucifer eventually wanted to be as God. You may wonder why Lucifer would want to rebel against God. He really had it made. He was God's premier angel, but he too had free will, and soon, iniquity, which included pride, was found in him. He began a rebellion, and there was war in heaven. Lucifer and one-third of the angels rose up against God, but no one can fight against God and win. Consequently, that rebellion was doomed to fail, and Lucifer and the rebellious angels were cast out of God's presence, down to earth. Here is a good example of what pride and rebellion against God will do to you. Anyone with any sense would know that you cannot war against God and have the slightest chance of winning. Listening to and taking part in any kind of rebellion against the almighty God, creator and sustainer of everything, is a lost cause. Those involved in such rebellion lose good sense. Those who listen to rebellion against God are foolish! Think about it. What kind of fool would ever even consider a possibility that rebellion against God will succeed? However, Lucifer, which was Satan's name at that time, and the rebellious angels, had a choice to make. They could have loved God or rebelled against God. You see, God wanted his creation to love him like he loved them. Those doing the loving must decide to love, and that requires free will. The rebels knew God, and that is important to know. They were not innocent creatures who were learning about God. They knew him, knew his power and authority, but were deceived by their leader, Lucifer. This rebellion was no contest. They were instantly cast out of heaven and onto the earth with no chance of returning. Since they did this with full knowledge of God and who he was, they could not say that God was unfair when he presented his plan to save man but did not make that plan available to the angels. The angels were fully mature when they rebelled. They knew God. Man was new to creation. Adam and Eve were babies in life and did not understand the ramifications of rebellion. Therefore, God was being fair to give man a chance for redemption

# The Creation of Man

When God created man, Satan was on this earth. However, God had given Adam (including Eve) complete authority over everything he had made on this earth. God told Adam that, on the day that they ate from the Tree of the Knowledge of Good and Evil, they would die. God didn't want Adam and Eve to come to the knowledge of evil, who is personified in Satan, until they had learned how to use their authority. But they rebelled against God when Satan, in the form of a snake, talked Eve into eating the fruit from the Tree of the Knowledge of Good and Evil and then convinced Adam into eating some also. Incidentally, Adam wasn't off in the garden somewhere while his wife was being tempted. The story says that, after Satan gave her the fruit to eat, "she gave some to her husband who was there with her, and he ate it." Adam was right there with Eve during this whole time, and he just let that snake fast-talk his wife into eating something that he knew would kill her. Eve was deceived by the snake, but Adam purposefully rebelled against God. Adam had authority over that snake and could have told it to leave.

Instead, he allowed that snake to tempt his wife, and then he, too, followed her into death. Do you remember there was also a Tree of Life in the garden? You may wonder why they could not just take a little bite from the Tree of Life and be alive again. That Tree of Life would have made Adam and Eve immortal in the flesh. However, if they had eaten of its fruit, they would have spent the rest of eternity with a spirit that was separated from God. And that is a definition of hell. Consequently, God banished them from the Garden of Eden and hid the garden for all time.

# The Death of Man

Many people have the wrong concept of death. Death does not mean no longer existing, because nothing becomes nonexistent; it just changes form. When you set fire to a piece of paper, it doesn't cease to exist. Its form is simply changed from paper to gas, smoke, and ashes. The parts separate from each other and dissipate into the air and the ground, but they do not cease to exist. God told Adam that he would die on the day he ate of the Tree of the Knowledge of Good and Evil. However, when he did, he didn't appear to die. He still had his body, he still had his soul, which includes his personality, reason, and other thought processes, so what died? Adam's and Eve's spirits died or became separated from God. As a result, their offspring were born with spirits that were dead or separated from God. Eventually, their bodies followed their spirits into death, and that set the stage for the fate of all mankind.

# The Redemption Plan

The Bible tells that "all have sinned and have come short of the glory of God." Since no one can come into the presence of the most holy God unless they are pure, we are all bound for hell, which is the eternal absence of God's presence. But God loved his man so much that he devised a plan of redemption. He couldn't just say "I forgive you. You guys just made a mistake. Come on back home." He couldn't do that because he banned Lucifer from his presence forever and did not forgive him. If God had just forgiven man, Satan could have gone to God and told him that he isn't fair. Remember, Satan wants to be as the Most High. However, if he can't ascend to the heights of God, he thought he would try to bring God down to his level. So man had to be cast from God's presence as Satan was. Man had to suffer the consequences of rebellion as Satan did. But God devised a great plan. Part of that plan included having man prepare sacrifices for his sins, which were then offered to God. These sacrifices allowed man's sins to be forgiven for a time, but man still had that dead spirit and would always continue to sin. In addition, man still had to suffer death—banishment from God's presence.

God had decided that "in the fullness of time," he would be born in a human body, live a perfect life, and would himself, once and for all, become the sacrifice, or the one who receives the punishment for the sins of man. He would accept the punishment for the sins of man and fulfill eternal justice. The Bible tells us that, since sin came into the world through the disobedience of one man, Adam, it is appropriate for salvation to come through the obedience of one man, Jesus. You may say that both Adam and Eve sinned, which is true. However, Genesis 1:27 says, "So God created man in his own image, in the image of God created he him; male and female created he them." Adam and Eve were the first of mankind and were created, not born. It was his creation, mankind, who sinned.

God had to come up with something because man cannot ever become good enough to enter into God's presence. No matter how hard he tries not to, man will always figure out a way to be rebellious against God. As a result of Adam's sin, he was born with a dead spirit. But Jesus said that we can come into God's presence if we become born again or receive a new spirit, one that is alive like Adam and Eve before they died. Now, remember who we claim Jesus to be. He is the Word of God made manifest in the flesh. He is the second person of the Godhead. If that is hard to understand, let me use an example. An apple is comprised of the skin, the meat, and the core. We still understand that it is an apple, but we know that it is three parts in nature. So it is with God. He is the Father, the Son, and the Holy Spirit. The Son, who is also called the Word of God, became flesh and accepted the punishment of death and banishment from God's presence as a man for us. However, since he was God in flesh form, death couldn't hold him, and he rose from the dead and ascended into heaven. Now, punishment for our sin is no longer over us, and we are free to be restored. Now we can have the dead spirit replaced by a spirit that can be joined with God.

# Receiving the Redemption

We now have an avenue by which we can get into heaven. That avenue is by accepting the sacrifice of Jesus, who died for our sins. How do we do that? By confessing that we believe Jesus is the Son of God, that he accepted the punishment of death for us, that he died for our sins, and that He rose again. When we do that with a sincere heart, we become born again. You may say, "I'm not dead, so I can't be born again." Ah, but you are dead. At least your spirit is dead, because you were born with a dead spirit, as is all mankind. When you "believe with your heart that Jesus is the Son of God and confess with your mouth that God raised him from the dead," as stated in the book of Romans, you become born again. Your spirit is born again, and you will now go to heaven when you die. This is the "born again" experience and happens in a moment, just like your first birth happened in a moment. Some think that, if you believe in Jesus, work real hard at being good, and try to not do too many bad things, you have a good chance of getting into heaven. In fact, a large portion of the church believes that lie. If being good enough on our own and doing a whole bunch of nice things can get us into heaven, then why do we need Jesus? No, believing in your heart that God raised Christ from the dead and confessing with your mouth that he is Lord is all you need to do to become born again. That is all you need to do to get into heaven. But there is more to being born again than getting to heaven. Since your spirit is now alive, you can commune with God. You can commune with the Almighty Creator and sustainer of this world!

# The New Nature

I have explained the problem with mankind and presented the solution. We now know that there is a way for us to be sure that we will go to heaven. If you aren't born again by the time you die, your spirit cannot be with God because it is dead or separated from God. You will exist forever in hell. Your chance to be with God forever is only available during your life here on earth.

# Born Again

So does that mean that, if I were born again, I will just have to muddle through life like everyone else, hoping that things go right? But if they don't, at least I'll go to heaven when I die? Absolutely not! Salvation is ongoing and begins the moment you are born again, not the moment you die. The Bible tells us in Romans 8:14 that "those who are led by the Spirit of God, they are the sons of God." The minute you were born again, you became a son of God, as stated in 2 Corinthians 5:17: "Old things have passed away, behold, all things are new." What is new? Your spirit is new! Remember, you are three parts in nature. Spirit, soul, and body. Your new spirit can now commune with God because it is alive, or joined with God. We often hear people say that, although we are born again, we still have the "old man" or our "old nature" to deal with, but that cannot possibly be true. If it were, we would be four parts in nature, not three. We would be new spirit, old spirit, soul, and body. In 2 Corinthians 5:17, it says, "Therefore if any man be in Christ, he is a new creature: old things are passed away: behold all things are become new." You become "in Christ" when you confess that Jesus is Lord and believe in your heart that God raised him from the dead. That is how we become born again. Your first birth was instantaneous, and so is

15

your second birth. This means that, when your body dies, your spirit will go to God That is what the Bible says, and it makes perfect sense to me based on my stated foundational beliefs.

Remember, when we become born again, we have become one with God. In 1 Corinthians 6:17, it says, "He who is joined unto the Lord is one spirit." That doesn't mean that now we are a creative God like he is or that we will create a universe to rule over. We are told that our body is the temple of the Holy Spirit. That means that the Spirit of God lives in us. We are one with him. I know that sounds strange, but it is fundamental Christianity. Does that mean that we will never sin again? No. That we will have it made from now on? No. That we will always make good decisions and that hard times won't come to us anymore? No, it doesn't. It does mean that we now have a God-given ability to resist sin, that we trust God to help us in times of need, and that we can be led by God to make right decisions. However, none of this comes automatically. We have to study God's Word, commune with God, and learn how to recognize his voice. And after all that, we have to follow his leading, let him teach us his Word, and grow in him. If this sounds familiar, it should. This is what Adam and Eve were supposed to do!

Becoming born again must be the first thing you do if you want to be successful in getting to know God. Without a new spirit that can commune with God, you will not get very far in your search for God. If you haven't been born again by now, this is a good time to receive Christ. Just put this book down, and tell God that you believe that Jesus took the punishment for your sins instead of you having to receive it. He was crucified, he died, he rose from the dead, and he ascended into heaven. If you believe that and will now confess that Jesus is your Lord, congratulations! You have a new spirit and are born again. If you have decided to not to do this, you may as well put this book down. It will make no sense to you.

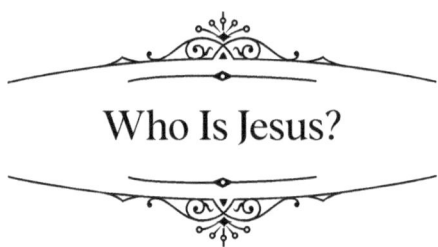

# Who Is Jesus?

While Jesus was on earth, he told his disciples that the time would come when he would die but that, after three days, he would rise from the dead. They didn't really understand what he was saying, but can you blame them? They could not really comprehend the fact that they were walking and talking with the God in the flesh. Do you remember that I showed you that God is three parts in nature— Father, Son, and Holy Spirit? Well, Jesus is the son of God, the second part of the three-part nature. The disciples were actually living with the God of the universe! However, they had dead spirits and, as a result, could not fully understand what was happening. They believed he was the Messiah, the redeemer spoken of in the scriptures, but they did not really know what that meant.

# A Promise from God

When Jesus died on the cross and rose from the dead, he appeared to his followers, taught them many things, and stayed with them for forty days. At the end of the forty days, Jesus ascended into heaven. However, before he left them, he told them to return to Jerusalem and wait for the promise of the Father. He told them that they would be baptized with the Holy Spirit, they would receive power after the Holy Spirit had come upon them, and that they were to wait until that happened. By this time, they were born again because they believed that Jesus had died in their place for their sins and he had risen from the dead. But before they did anything about being born again, they were to wait for the power from the Holy Spirit. They didn't know what that meant, but they knew that they had better wait.

Based on my foundational belief system, as stated earlier, that the Bible is God's Word, this whole thing makes perfect sense to me. However, if I did not have this foundational belief system, the next phase in this plan would sound very strange.

# The Baptism with the Holy Spirit and Speaking in Tongues

Jesus knew that, as his disciples began spreading this wonderful news through the land, they would quickly come upon stiff resistance. They had this new spirit, which allowed them to live forever with God, but they needed power from on high when the resistance to this great news was preached. So they all got together in Jerusalem, in this large room, as he had told them to do, and waited and prayed. There were about 120 people in that room all praying and all in one accord—meaning, they were unified—when suddenly there was a sound from heaven as if it were a rushing mighty wind, according to Acts 2:2. Then there appeared what looked like tongues of fire sitting on each of them, and they were all filled with the Holy Spirit and began speaking in other tongues, or languages.

# What Is Speaking in Other Tongues?

The scripture in 1 Corinthians 14:14–15 shows us that praying in tongues is what is known as praying in the spirit. The apostle Paul said that, when you pray in tongues, your spirit prays but your mind does not know what you are saying. You are praying in the language of the angels and praying unto God. I think that praying in tongues is a logical and very useful gift for God to give us. It isn't something we learn but is given to us when we receive the baptism with the Holy Spirit.

If you are born again, you need the baptism with the Holy Spirit so that you can live your new life in the power of God. If the first followers of Jesus needed that power, the rest of us need it also. The Bible tells us that praying in the Spirit—that is, praying in tongues —"builds up our most holy faith." You have probably found out by now that there are times when you need your faith built up. Praying in tongues builds up your faith. How do you get this gift? You simply ask God to baptize you with the Holy Spirit. If you are a born-again Christian, you can have it right now. You can stop reading; get to a nice, quiet place; calm your thoughts; settle down; and ask God to baptize you with his Holy Spirit. After you have received the baptism, you will be able to speak in tongues. After you have asked, start praising God and thanking him for his great goodness. Then stop speaking in your native language, but keep on talking. You will be speaking in the tongues of angels and will get more proficient at this new language as you speak. God will give you this gift, but he will not make you talk. You have to do the speaking. This isn't spooky or weird. Remember, it is just logical for God to allow you to speak in the tongues of angels. After all, you have a new spirit; you should be able to speak in the language of the angels. Another way to receive the baptism of the Holy Spirit is to have someone pray for you, which is the most common way. In any case, you will need this gift as you continue your Christian walk.

# The Second Chapter of Acts Experience

In the book of Acts, the second chapter, we see that, when those 120 people in the upper room began speaking in tongues, everyone around them was amazed. Since this was the day of Pentecost, there were people in town from many other countries, with many other languages.

The Bible lists sixteen other nations represented, all with their own languages. Many people heard the wonders of God proclaimed in their native language. Now remember, tongues is the language of angels, not any earthly language. However, three times the Bible says that the people heard the gospel being preached in their own language. A closer look at these verses shows us that never do they say that those in the upper room were speaking in those different languages. It says the people heard what was being said in their native tongue. Those speaking with other tongues were speaking the languages of the angels, and God translated those words into the languages of those who were in the crowd. This is obvious when you read the second chapter of Acts. Some of the listeners mocked what was being said and thought that those speaking were just drunk. Those people heard the 120 speaking in the tongues of angels, and to them it was unintelligible and garbled, not just some other language. So they thought that those people who were speaking were drunk. They were hearing men speaking in the tongues of angels. They wouldn't have thought that all these speakers were drunk if the 120 were actually speaking in all those foreign languages. They would have believed they were witnessing a major miracle!

Peter then stood up and told the crowd that those speakers were not drunk but were fulfilling the prophecy of the prophet Joel. He went on to preach the gospel, and when he had finished, about three thousand people were converted to Christianity. Do you suppose all that would have happened if Peter had not been baptized with the Holy Spirit? Absolutely not! If Peter and the others needed that power to be effective, you will need that power also.

Okay, you have received Christ as Savior and now have a new spirit. You are born again. You have also received the baptism with the Holy Spirit and speak with the tongues of angels. Don't think that you have finally arrived. You have just started and are ready to live this new life filled with power. So life is great and everything is going to be wonderful from now on! Right.

# The Battle

There is a battle raging, as we speak, and it is violent and vicious. That battle is all around us and has been going on since the beginning. We were born into the middle of this battle, and as a result, we just think that this is how life is supposed to be. This is a battle in the spiritual realm and has drastically affected all life. Its end result is death itself and is sometimes called the battle between good and evil or between good spirits and evil spirits or even between God and the devil. However, that is not who is waging the war. This battle is between Satan and his forces and mankind. Satan isn't in a battle with God. If he were, he would be dispatched immediately as he was in his attempted rebellion against God. Satan doesn't stand a chance against God, and he knows it. We are the ones at war with Satan and his demons. All the world's problems are a result of this war that has been going on since Adam and Eve sinned. The sad thing is most of us don't even know it. We think that this is just life. You may say that we aren't in a battle, but we are, and Satan is beating us up. He is making us sick, tempting us with evil, stealing our money, and causing depression, fear, and doubt.

All these have been part of our lives since we were born, and we believe that this is just the way it goes. But this is not the way it is supposed to go. Jesus said that the thief comes to kill, steal, and destroy but that he (Jesus) came to give us abundant life. Isn't it obvious that what most of us have been living is a bit short of an abundant life? People believe that God will make us sick, or take good things away from us or cause us to live in poverty to teach us something. It doesn't make sense to believe that God is causing all this trouble to teach us something. He is called our loving Father, and the Bible says that he cares for us. If you believe that sickness is sent by God to teach you something, you had better not go to a doctor to get healed or take any medication to get well. You had better find out what God is trying to teach you and learn from it. You don't want to be going against God's will and getting healed before you learn what God wants to teach you. Now, doesn't that sound ridiculous? Of course it does! What is really happening is that Satan is doing his best to steal, kill, and destroy, and he is doing a pretty good job of it!

# Our Weapons

"The weapons of our warfare are not carnal but mighty through God." Your weapons are "the sword of the Spirit which is the Word of God" and "praying in the spirit," as seen in Ephesians 6:17–18. The earlier passages define what your armor is. It is obvious that, if our battle were with spiritual forces, we will need spiritual weapons. It is also obvious that, if we were told what our weapons and armor are, we must be in a battle.

Since I believe that the Bible is the Word of God and all this warfare stuff is described in detail in the Bible, it behooves me to read, study, and meditate on the Bible. Remember, the Word of God is called a spiritual sword. In today's world, the weapon would be called our assault rifle. It is what we use when we attack the enemy. That means we are to go on the offensive. We have to fight. No good soldier goes to war not knowing how to use his weapon. He practices with it and gets to know it inside and out. He becomes proficient with it and can pick it up and use it without a moment's notice.

I know that some don't like to fight. They just want to take it easy and be "peaceful." Unfortunately, the only way to leave the battle is to give up and be captured. You are in a battle, whether you like it or not. Giving up is not an option. When this enemy captures you, he keeps you under his boot, kicking and beating on you until the day you die. He will destroy everything about you if you let him. However, unlike fleshly battles, the Bible guarantees that you will be the winner if you just follow the instructions in the Bible—the Word of God.

# The Sword of the Spirit

Going into battle knowing for certain that you will win is pretty motivating. It almost makes the battle fun! At the very least, all fear of failing is gone, and you can get started without fear nagging you. Oh sure, any fight is stressful while you are in the middle of it. However, every time you get through a battle, you are more encouraged and ready for the next one. Once you see how well this sword of the Spirit works, you will get through your battles with fewer nicks and cuts. And the more you use the sword, the better fighter you become and the farther you advance.

OK, you've got a nice sword and are guaranteed a win if you use it. Now what? Where is this sword, and how do you learn to go to battle with it? The Bible tells us that this sword is called the "sword of the Spirit" and is the Word of God. The Bible also says that "we battle not against flesh and blood but against principalities and powers and evil wickedness in high places." Although it may look like our problems are corning from a person or people, the truth is these problems, which are our battle, are coming from the spiritual realm. Remember how we discovered that Satan had been cast to earth and tempted Eve in the form of a snake? When Satan rebelled against God, he convinced one-third of the angels to rebel with him, and they were cast from God's presence onto the earth also. So Satan and one-third of the original angels are on this earth now. Is it any wonder that there is so much destruction, sorrow, and death here? Adam and Eve, as representatives of mankind, were given authority over the earth and were told to be fruitful and multiply. That authority was not taken from them when they rebelled. They still had authority over the earth and, in effect, were told by God to manage the earth. However, the Bible tells us that we become a slave to the one to whom we yield ourselves. What we have now is Satan, to whom Adam and Eve yielded themselves using the authority that was given to man. Satan does not have any authority on this earth except for that which man will give him! I know that sounds strange, but based on everything previously stated, it makes absolute sense. When you get a revelation of this truth, it will completely change the way you pray. One thing you will realize is that, since God gave you authority on this earth, you must resist ungodly temptation instead of asking God to remove it. He won't remove it because it is up to you to resist it. The Bible tells us to resist the devil, and he will flee from you.

# The Battle against Temptation

Temptation comes to you to do something that you know isn't godly. This is Satan's work, and he has put this temptation in front of you, and you are fighting against it with all your might. However, it is getting harder and harder to resist, and soon, you fall. You promise God that you will do better next time, but when next time comes, you fall again. This goes on over and over with a number of situations. As time goes by, this problem becomes a part of your life. You get more and more discouraged because you keep failing. You finally become completely neutralized, and you give up. At that point, you can't get anything done for God, and you wonder why God doesn't help you.

Sometimes you are unable to resist temptation because of evil spiritual activity in your life. Sometimes you have developed a bad habit. Sometimes there are people in your life who are listening to evil spirits and doing things that cause you trouble. Here are examples:

*The problem*: You can't stop drinking alcohol. This is a common problem and is usually caused by evil spirits' activity in your life. It is also a bad habit and is helped on by the people you hang around with.

*The solution*: Remember, the Word of God is your weapon. The Word says to resist the devil, and he will flee from you. You swing the sword by saying "I resist you, devil, and you flee from me." You say this as often as you must until the power of the temptation is gone. Then you begin thanking God for deliverance and praising God for his mercy. I can guarantee that you won't start drinking while you are praising God. The temptation to drink will probably come again because it has also become a habit. However, you will notice that it isn't so irresistible. That is because the evil spirit pushing it has been stopped. During this time of temptation, you thank God for deliverance and praise him some more. Most habits can be broken within one month if you will stick with it. The temptation will continue to come again, off and on, but you will realize that you can resist it if you so desire. Here is where the sword of the Spirit, the Word of God, helps you to continue to live free from this temptation. You speak to temptation when it comes and command it to leave. You say something like this:

> Because Jesus is my Lord, I have the Spirit of God inside me, and I am one with the Father. Jesus has delivered me from all the power of the enemy, and I have been given authority over all of the enemy's power. Therefore, nothing by any means will harm me. I tread on serpents and scorpions (demon activity), and the temptation to drink alcohol leaves me now.

Although you have been delivered from this temptation's irresistible power, it will still try to come back. It may just be by the force of habit or by the influence of some evil spirit. However, it will not be irresistible. Proclaim to the heavens that you have the fruit of the Spirit, which includes self-control. Satan cannot keep pushing you to drink forever. Although it may seem like this battle is going on forever, Satan doesn't have the patience to continue for too long. Patience is a fruit of the Spirit, and he doesn't have the fruit of the Spirit. He will go off to bother someone else for a while. You will find that, as time goes by, you really don't want to take a drink, but then your old drinking buddies try to get you to go out with them. By now, the power of that temptation to drink is gone, and you let your guard down. You think, *Man, I really have beaten this. I can go out with the guys tonight and not fear that I will get drunk.* This is a dangerous thought, and the Bible compares this to a dog that goes back to its vomit. Once you are free, stay free!

I have just described spiritual battle. The situation just mentioned is how this war is going on. As you can see, you've been in this battle all along but just haven't known it. You have probably been kicked around and bruised a number of times. You have probably even won a battle or two. By understanding what is really happening and how to use your spiritual weapon, you can now win all the battles all the time and with a lot less trouble. It is sure nice to know that it is possible to win all the time.

# The Armor

All soldiers involved in battle must have armor. Since we are involved in a spiritual battle, we need spiritual armor. You cannot go into a battle with just a sword. You are bound to be shot at, stabbed at, and otherwise attacked by the enemy you are fighting. Incidentally, while we are discussing being attacked, let's be sure to take care of our wounded. When one of our soldiers gets hit and falls, let's not just finish him off right there on the battlefield. Let's take him back from the front lines, dress his wounds, and let him heal. He isn't our enemy. He is a brother who got waylaid by the enemy. Let's be merciful. Remember, on the first page of this book, I talked about sowing and reaping; you know, what goes around comes around. You may fall sometimes and need mercy and help. What you give out will come back to you.

The Bible tells us in Ephesians 6:10–8 what the spiritual armor is. It is the belt of truth, the breastplate of righteousness, your feet fitted with readiness of the gospel, the shield of faith, and the helmet of salvation. Outfit yourself with this armor. I'll say it again. Put on the armor of God! No good soldier goes into battle without his armor. If you try, you are going to get hurt. God didn't give you this armor just to make you look cool. He made it to protect you. So wear it! Look at what God says this armor is. Read the scripture in Ephesians chapter 6 for a good description of your armor. Like any good soldier, you will exercise, get plenty of rest, and practice with your sword. Exercise by staying in good spiritual condition. Rest by not being too hard on yourself. Take it easy, and don't fight all the time. Everyone needs a little break. That doesn't mean that there are times when you just stop fellowshipping with other Christians or decide to go a few weeks without reading God's Word. It may mean that, instead of intensely studying the Word, you simply read it like you would an interesting story. You practice with your sword by attacking something simple. Instead of getting into fasting and intense prayer for God to save the world, you start out by telling your neighbor about your salvation experience. Like anything else, start out slowly until you become proficient with your sword and know how to let your armor protect you.

# Community

**D**o not be deceived; you need the community of Christians. You cannot make it by yourself. You are never going to be effective trying to live the Christian life by yourself. When you were born again, you were given a new spirit in place of the old dead spirit. However, another thing happened to you in the spiritual realm. Colossians 1:13 says that God delivered you from the power of darkness and into the kingdom of God's son. You were given a new residence, and that residence is Jesus's kingdom. You have a new home. Read the first chapter of Colossians a few times, and let this description of what happened to you sink in. Meditate on some of the verses that jump out at you. Here is an important thing to remember when reading the Bible. This book is the living Word of God. There is life in its pages. You can read the same passage over and over at different times for years, and one day, it just jumps out of the pages and into your heart, and you are never the same again. When that happens to you, you will never again look at God's Word as just a book. It isn't called the Book of Life for nothing.

Find a church home as soon as you can. Don't wander out there in the battlefield alone. You have probably found out by now that it isn't safe out there. You need someone to watch your back! Hebrews 10:5 says that we should not forsake the assembling of ourselves together with one another. Don't just go into the first building you see that has a cross on it. There are a large number of churches that are filled with people, including their pastors, who are not Christians. Look for a church that advertises itself as a Bible-believing church. Pray to God, and ask him to lead you. Remember, Romans 8:14 says "that as many as are led by the Spirit of God, they are the sons of God." Here is a good chance to wield the sword of the spirit, which is the Word of God. You pray and ask God to lead you to the church that is best for you, and then you say, "I am a son of God, and therefore, I am led by the Spirit of God." You have just swung your sword at whatever could have hindered you from finding a church. Although you may not see anything, you hit your target, and God will lead you to the church you need. You can use that sword against anything the enemy throws against you, so get proficient with it!

You have just read a beginner's summary of Christian life. My prayer for you is that you make a decision to go forward, and as stated in Matthew 6:33, "Seek ye first the kingdom of God, and his righteousness; and all these things shall be added unto you."

# About the Author

I am married to my wonderful wife, Donna, have four grown children and five grandchildren, and currently live in Mesa, Arizona.

I received Jesus as my Savior nearly fifty years ago through the ministry of Campus Crusade for Christ and have ministered in a few different areas. Early on, I was a member of a small Christian band that ministered in churches and other Christian organizations. I also ministered solo and wrote the songs I sang.

I was part of the worship team for a church in Arizona and was called to pastor two of their mission churches.

My desire is to get Christians to take their belief in Christ seriously enough so that they take every opportunity to present the truth of Jesus to whomever they can. Jesus is returning soon, and we have to do what he has called us to do—that is, to present the gospel whenever we can. In order to do that effectively, we have to have a good understanding of who God is and how he operates. We have to be able to present this information to people in a way that makes sense. This booklet presents the gospel in such a logical way that a serious seeker of the truth will only have one choice, and that is to receive Christ as their Savior.